This Book Belongs To:

_____

A Message To You Queen:

This poem came to me in the middle of the night. I'd run away to another city to be near the ocean, trying to get away from my pain only to have an encounter with Papa. That's my name for "God."

It was a cold November night; the hotel room was dark and cold because I opened the door leading to the balcony to hear the ocean waves. I still remember the large tears running down my face as I grabbed my cell phone and typed this poem in the body of an email.

As I poured my heart out to Papa, I was excited because He began to speak back! He told me about my worth and His thoughts toward me. Queen, you are a daughter of the King. And I know that you may have experienced hurt, but God WANTS to heal you right where you hurt. He is there for the asking, and get this...He is The Bodyguard of Your Heart! That means that sometimes He will say, "No," to things you desire because it isn't FOR you. What does that mean? It means that sometimes rejection really is protection.

Queen, you are so enough. As a matter of fact, you are MORE THAN ENOUGH, and I pray that as you read my conversation with Papa that your enoughness resonates with you as it did with me.

Tamika Hall

I remember meeting
The Bodyguard for
the first time.
Taking my hand,
His touch was gentle,
His voice was kind.

Normally,
I'd be weary of someone
in my space.
He appeared out nowhere,
yet didn't seem out of place.

His presence cut through
the shadows
of my never-ending night,
but here He was
surrounded by light.

I instantly felt a
connection to Him.
In one body
He was a father, a brother,
and even a friend.

"So, why are you here?"
Was the question I had.
To which He replied,
"Your Help Wanted AD."

He handed me a scroll
that rolled out past feet.
On it were my hopes,
failed dreams,
and goals I didn't meet.

Relationships that rendered
my heart shattered
and defeated,
toxic decisions
that left me depleted.

I must admit
I was taken aback.
Those were my thoughts...
but I never posted that.

See...this is the reason
my heart needed to be hard.
Why I keep to myself
and never trust anyone.

"Who betrayed me?"
I thought,
"Who told Him my secrets
and fears?"
As if hearing my questions,
"It's your writing,"
He answered,
"It was written in tears."

"In the middle of the night
you cried when no one
could see,
But your tears were
collected and delivered to Me."

Finally, I understood,
imagine my surprise,
"That's right, I Am God,
now see yourself
through MY EYES."

"You're peculiar,
royal, and very unique,
you are marvelously complex,
my favorite masterpiece."

Jokingly I said,
"You make it seem like
I'm a piece of art."'
He paused then said,
"Don't you understand I'm
The Bodyguard Of Your Heart?"

The confusion on my face
was plain to see.
Patiently, God began
to break it down for me.

"Where you go I go,
I'm always by your side.
As your Bodyguard,
I watch your front, your back,
and protect you from
dangers that hide."

"I'll survey a land,
search a person,
before you arrive there,
remove threats
seen and unseen,
most times you're not aware."

"You've been upset
for the times I said, 'No,'
I wasn't punishing you,
but you were aiming too low."

"You are not to be wasted, devalued, or treated like a thing, or don't you know, you're the daughter of The King?"

"I'm too nice,
I love too hard,
that's what you say,
But my daughter -
I made you that way."

"I created you to be
different,
to see life through
a different lens,
That's why when others
may break,
you just bend."

"You were created
to love,
It sets you apart,
I handcrafted you
to have that
big heart."

"That's why you
must forgive.
Forgiveness allows
you to be free
It unlocks doors to
purpose and destiny."

"You're anointed and appointed,
You were born to be more.
When the storms
of life rage
Like an eagle you catch
the wind and soar."

"High above problems
Over naysayers and hate,
Right now they may laugh,
But daughter you were
designed to be great."

"Many times you've been hurt,
and there is much
you have lost,
My child I can't wait to restore
the fragments of your heart."

"It's happening right now,
you may not feel it
and not yet see,
but it will be evident as
you turn your pain over to me."

I looked at Him,
tears pouring from my eyes,
I tried to speak,
all I could do was cry.

**Frustrated, I crumbled
to my knees,
my sobs were loud,
my tears drowning His feet.**

On one hand, I felt broken,
on the other complete.
"Open your eyes," He said,
"It's time for you to see."

I was in a closet,
baggage and boxes
covered every part.
"Where am I?" I asked.
He replied,
"This is your broken heart."

"Every time you felt shattered,
tattered, and torn,
you packed the pieces in this closet,
and a callous was born."

"That hardness makes it hard
to give and be loved,
You can't hear me clearly,
If you're holding a grudge."

"You've been betrayed,
people used you for their gain,
just give them to me,
I'll replace your
shame with praise."

So, I gave Him my baggage
I didn't even look inside,
the boxes were heavy for me,
but for Him they were light.

Years of anguish released,
right then and there.
I wept on His feet,
and dried them with my hair.

"You're never alone,
I'm always near,
every detail of your day
I want to hear.
Now stand with confidence
and know I'm not far,
that's because I'm
The Bodyguard of Your Heart."

Connect / Book
Dr. Tamika Hall

Dr. Tamika Hall is available for ministry engagements.

info@tamikahall.com
www.tamikahall.com